The Illinois Guide Book To Auto Accidents And Injuries

Steve Giacoletto
Personal Injury Lawyer

Copyright © 2013 Steve Giacoletto

All rights reserved.

ISBN: 1490513841
ISBN-13: 978-1490513843
Library of Congress Control Number: 2013911606

All rights reserved. No portion of the publication may be reproduced, stored in any retrieval system, or transmitted in any form by any means—electronic, photocopying, editing or any other—except for brief quotation in printed reviews, without the prior written permission of the author, Steve C. Giacoletto.

This Book May Be for You If You:

1. Were **injured in an accident** involving a car, truck, motor cycle, bus or any other moving vehicle.
2. Do not think you were more than more than 50% at fault for the accident.
3. Have, or will probably have, **medical bills** of more than $2,000 from the accident.
4. Are not bothered about having your damages paid by a **multi-billion dollar** insurance company.

If you can answer YES to each of these questions then contact us at:
Giacoletto Law Firm
1601 Vandalia Street Collinsville, IL 62234
Phone: (618) 346-8841
Toll Free: (866) 346-8841
Fax: (618) 346-8843
sgiacoletto@scglawoffice.com
www.scglawoffice.com

CONTENTS

1. You've Been in an Accident ... Now What? — 1
2. Quick Tips — 2
3. Should You Talk to the Other Driver's Insurance Company? — 4
4. Do You Have to Talk to Your Own Insurance Companies — 5
5. How Insurance Companies Value Your Claim — 7
6. Medical Treatment after Your Acciden — 8
7. How Do You Get Your Medical Bills Paid? — 11
8. Use Your Auto Insurance to Pay Your Medical Bills — 14
9. Do You Have to Reimburse Your Own Insurance Companies? — 16
10. Getting Your Car Fixed — 17

11.	Your Car Is Totaled; You Still Owe Money on It	19
12.	What if the Other Driver Has No Auto Insurance?	21
13.	What if You Don't Have Auto Insurance?	23
14.	Photographs and Witnesses	24
15.	What Is Your Case Worth?	25
16.	How Long Will Your Case Take?	26
17.	Do You Have to Settle Your Case?	27
18.	Do You Have to Go to Trial? With a Jury?	28
19.	Drunk Driver Accidents	29
20.	Criminal Charges Against the Drunk Driver	30
21.	What Happens if a Minor Was Hurt in the Accident?	31
22.	Statutes of Limitations Can Stop Your Claim	32

23.	What Are the Damages in your Case?	34
24.	What You Must Know about Insurance Companies	35
25.	Do You really Need a Lawyer for Your Accident Case?	37
26.	How Do You Pay a Lawyer to Take Your Case?	39
27.	Should You Tell Your Lawyer Everything about Your Case?	41
28.	At least 12 Things You Should Expect from Your Lawyer	42
29.	Five Things You Normally Won't Be Told about Lawyers	43
30.	Are People These Days Too Lawsuit Happy?	45
31.	This Book Does Not Offer Legal Advice	46
32.	The Ten Worst Insurance Companies in America and the Wealth of the Insurance Industry	47
33.	About the Author	49

1
You've Been in an Accident ... Now What?

If you're reading this book, you or a loved one has probably been in an auto accident and are now forced to participate in the often and always frustrating world of personal injury law. The good news is that this inevitable confusion and frustration can be minimized by educating yourself on the basics of the how the legal and insurance processes work once you've been in an accident.

This book is not meant to have all the answers about your accident case, but it will give you a good starting point as to where you stand with the insurance companies, why you might need a lawyer, and if you do, what kind of questions and expectations you may have for your lawyer. And don't be afraid to ask your lawyer a lot of questions. Every lawyer has a natural instinct to want to teach other people what they've learned about injury cases over their many years of practice. Not only that, it's your lawyer's ethical duty to answer your questions as best they are able to do so.

At this point, the most important thing that you do is read on, get educated, and then act upon what you've learned. And by the end of this book, you'll know what kind of lawyer to call and you'll have a good idea of what to expect out of your claim. The biggest mistake you can make with your accident case is to do nothing and simply wait to see what the insurance comes up with for you.

2
Quick Tips

1. If you've been injured in an accident, **seek immediate medical treatment**. Or if at first you didn't think you were injured, but now believe you might have been, seek medical attention as soon as possible.
2. **Do not talk** to or correspond with the other driver's insurance company about the accident or your injuries.
3. **Do not sign** any forms for the other driver's insurance company.
4. Be extremely careful of what you post on Facebook, Twitter, or any other social media sites. The insurance company and their lawyers will review your postings for anything they think will help minimize your injuries and lessen your damages.
5. Don't be in a hurry to settle your accident claim.
6. The insurance companies and their employees are not your friends, even if they're from your own insurance company.
7. Hire a lawyer that is **experienced in accident cases** as soon as possible.
8. Especially if you've been in an accident involving a big semi-truck, you would want a lawyer on the case the minute after it happened.
9. **Take pictures** of the vehicles in the accident and the surrounding area of the accident.
10. Take pictures of all your injuries from the accident.
11. **Keep all records** related to your accident from the moment it happens.
12. There's no reason to exaggerate your injuries.

13. Report the accident to your own insurance company. Use your own insurance company to help get your car repaired and get a rental car while yours is being fixed. If you don't have insurance, limit your conversations with the other driver's insurance company to getting your car fixed and obtaining a rental vehicle. Better yet, ask your lawyer to help you with getting your car repaired.

3
Should You Talk to the Other Driver's Insurance Company?

NO, NO, and NO.

That's why this chapter is so short; there are simply not enough good reasons for you to talk to the other driver's insurance company about your accident without first having hired a lawyer.

After your accident you will have at least two insurance companies wanting the details and to take your statement. One is your own insurance company; the other is the insurance company for the driver of the other vehicle. **Do not talk or correspond with the other driver's insurance company.** The only exception would be if you have no auto insurance for yourself, but still want the other driver's insurance to pay for your car repairs. For the extremely limited purpose of getting your car fixed or deciding its value if it was totaled, you want to avoid the insurance company for the driver who caused the accident. And even under these limited circumstances it is hazardous to your property claim to talk with the other driver's insurance company.

4
Do You Have to Talk to Your Own Insurance Companies?

Yes, for the most part you are obligated by your policies to cooperate with your own auto and health insurance companies. Still, do not think that your own insurance company is your friend and will look out for your best interest. No insurance company is your friend. The good news is that it is easier to deal with your own insurance companies than it is with the other driver's insurance company.

You can file a claim over the internet with most insurance companies, but at the very least their website will have a telephone number you can call to get your claim started. If you are not used to computers, you can send a copy of the Crash Report to your own insurance agent and ask him to start your claim. Your agent should report this claim to your insurance company on your behalf and your company should then contact the insurance company for the driver at fault.

If you do not have an insurance agent, or if the agent fails to report your claim because you have not heard from your insurance company within a couple of days, then contact your auto insurance company yourself to report the accident.

Even though you did not cause this accident, you need your insurance company to do four things:

1. Help get your car fixed; or if it's totaled, they pay for it at its fair market value.
2. Help you get a rental car while your car is being repaired.

3. Arrange for payment of some of your medical bills, if you have that type of coverage available.

Unlike dealing with the driver at fault's insurance company, you need to give your full cooperation to your own insurance company. If you don't then your insurance company may deny you coverage. If <u>your insurance company</u> needs a statement about the accident, then give them one, but have your lawyer present. If they need records, information or authorizations signed to get your doctor's records and bills, then you will probably have to give them one. However, you need to only release medical records and bills related to the accident. Normally, you should not have to give your auto insurance company access to all of your medical records for treatment prior to the accident.

5
How Insurance Companies Value Your Claim

About 70% of the auto accident cases are valued by insurance companies using an extremely expensive and complex computer program to determine the value of your claim. This computer program and others like it are commonly known as Colossus. Of the top 20 insurance companies in the United States, 16 of them use computer programs like Colossus as a way of saving them money by standardizing your injuries right along with everyone else's in the country. There are over 300 insurance companies thought to use Colossus-like programs; but good luck getting an insurance adjuster to admit that they'll be using it to evaluate your claim.

It used to be that normal people for the insurance companies made judgment calls based on common sense and human experience as to the value of the injuries to their fellow man. Now, data about your injuries, medical treatment, lost wages, expenses, etc. are plugged into a computer program that spits out a range of values on your claim. That's how most insurance adjusters settle injury cases these days. Still, many, if not most, injury lawyers have no idea about the existence of the Colossus program, much less how it works. So it's vital to get the insurance adjuster to look at the kind of data the Colossus program considers important in valuing your claim. For that, you'll need not only an experienced personal injury lawyer, but one who knows how to the beat the insurance company at its own game.

6
Medical Treatment after Your Accident

Emergency Room
If you've ever been in an accident you may have felt the need to make an immediate trip to the emergency room or a nearby doctor's office. If you've been to the emergency room, hopefully you made sure that the admissions office, attending nurse and treating physician were aware of **all your symptoms**. All too often doctors will treat the most obvious injury and give only minor attention to a patient's secondary aches and pains. If it's not the primary injury, many emergency room records will not show the complaints about a patient's headaches, sore neck, low back pain or a bruised knee. A sore neck can be a symptom of a rotator cuff tear. Low back pain could be from a bulging or herniated disc that may be chronic for years. A bruised knee could be from a torn ligament that requires surgery months later because it has no real chance of healing without dramatic intervention. It is very common that the secondary aches and pains are the ones that will give you problems for the months and years to come, long after the cuts and bruises are gone. Even though the emergency room doctors may not have treated what might be relatively minor injuries, you at least want on all your complaints mentioned in the medical records.

Family Physician
After you've been to the emergency room you'll want to follow-up with your family doctor to get treated for **all of your injuries** caused by the accident. If you have not been to the emergency room and your family physician is the first doctor treating your injuries, then make sure they address all of your aches and pains. Perhaps even more important than

in the emergency room, now is the time that you want to stress all of your symptoms for treatment by your doctor. Do not let your family doctor focus simply on taking stitches out of a cut or quickly looking at bruises left by the seat belt across your chest. If you are still in pain and having problems with your neck, low back, knee or any other part of your body, now is the time to relay those symptoms to your family doctor and have them treated as aggressively as permitted by the medical standards.

At this initial visit it may be that your family doctor does nothing more than some anti-inflammatory prescriptions, pain medication, or exercises to do at home. That is fine, if that is what the doctor orders. You just have to make sure he is aware of your symptoms and to what degree they are bothering you. For example, your low back hurts so much that you cannot get out of bed in the morning; or your knee hurts enough that you end up with a limp by the end of the day; or if your neck hurts so much that you cannot turn your head from side to side. Tell him all of your injury symptoms and give him as many examples as possible of the things that you cannot do.

Your doctor may decide that he needs to write you a prescription, set you up with physical therapy, or even refer you to a specialist. If so, make that appointment with the physical therapist or specialist as soon as possible. Just like with the emergency room doctor or your family physician, make sure your specialist is aware of all of your symptoms and limitations that you think were caused by the accident.

But do not expect your lawyer to refer you to a doctor. If your accident ends up going to a lawsuit, or even if it does not, it is damaging to your case to later read in the doctor's medical records that you were referred to his office by your lawyer. If your lawyer does need to refer you to a doctor or a specialist, discuss this matter with him in advance. If at all possible, you do not want your lawyer's name showing up in your medical records as the referring source

7
How Do You Get Your Medical Bills Paid?

Understand this: It is rare for the driver at fault's insurance company to pay your medical bills. If they do, it's probably because they're taking advantage of you and want to close out your file as soon as possible. Or, because you have such a good claim they're trying to keep you happy so you don't hire a lawyer and are hoping you will just go away.

Besides out of your own pocket, the first way to get your medical bills paid is from your medical payment coverage from **your own automobile insurance policy**. If you go to the hospital or doctor for treatment, give them your auto insurance card for so they know where to send bills for payment for your medical treatment.

The second first way to get your medical bills paid is with **your health insurance card**, if you have one. At the hospital or doctor's office, give them your health insurance card right along with your auto insurance card.

The third way to get your medical bills paid may be from a **state issued medical card**, if you are eligible. Typically, hospitals, doctors and physical therapists, and any other health care provider will not be overjoyed to take your state medical card. The reason is that health care providers that accept a state medical card are paid on a very low percentage compared to what their services are billed. However, when it comes time to get paid on your case, your state medical card is good for you because that means there will be less money taken from you to reimburse the state for paying your medical bills.

The fourth way to get your medical bills paid is through the **federal Medicare program**, if you are eligible. This program operates much in the same fashion as your state card issued medical card, but with more healthcare providers to choose from. In addition, Medicare may pay your doctors and hospitals quicker and at a higher percentage of their bills than does the state medical programs. On the flip side, by time you receive Medicare there will be a lien against your settlement proceeds that will make the insurance companies very nervous about paying you for your damages until that lien is resolved. Getting that lien resolved from Medicare is no easy task and can be very time consuming even under the best circumstances.

Even if you do not have any of the payment resources mentioned above, all is still not lost. Your lawyer should be able to recommend doctors that will treat you for your injuries without insurance or government assistance. These doctors will take a lien against the proceeds in your case to pay for your treatment. Remember though, even if your lawyer helps you find a doctor, you still don't want his name being in your medical records as the person that referred you to that doctor.

Keep in mind that hospitals, doctors, government assistance programs, and sometimes even insurance companies will have liens against your settlement or trial award. While it's typically near impossible for an individual to get these liens significantly lowered, your lawyer may be able to get those medical liens reduced.

One last point about getting your medical bills paid. In most states, it will not be legal or ethical for your attorney to pay your bills or loan you money for any reason. Your lawyer may be able to direct you to banks or lenders that can give you small loans to hold you over and then take a lien on the proceeds of your case. But be extremely careful before you take this desperate step. The interest rate on these types of loans is outrageously high and at times can make it difficult for your case to settle even when you're being made a fair offer.

8
Use Your Auto Insurance to Pay Your Medical Bills

One area that your insurance company is typically cooperative is medical payment coverage. In some policies, this is called Med Pay Coverage or Personal Injury Protection (PIP). When you bought your insurance policy, more than likely your agent sold you the medical payment coverage without you even knowing it. This type of coverage is similar to having a little bit of health insurance when it comes to having an accident in one of the insured cars. The cost for this type of coverage is fairly cheap and you probably would not have even noticed them on your auto insurance premiums invoice. To find out if you have medical payment coverage, or PIP, simply pull out your automobile insurance coverage statement and look for the words "medical payment coverage", "med pay", PIP, or something similar to those words.

Med Pay amounts are typically $500, $1,000, $2,000, $5,000 or $10,000. You could even have upwards of $25,000 of coverage. Whatever the coverage amount you have paid premiums for, this is the same amount that your insurance company will pay, per person, for medical bills in any accident that the insured car was involved in. This includes your own medical bills. Medical payment coverage will kick in, no matter who is at fault for the accident, including your own. Some PIP coverage even pays for lost wages.

When you go to your family doctor, physical therapy, a specialist, etc., make sure that they have your automobile insurance information on file so that they can submit their bills directly to the insurance company under your medical payment coverage claim. Doctors, physical therapists and specialists are typically happy to see you and treat your injuries so long as they know they are going to be paid. If you have health insurance, they will be doubly happy.

Despite all of this, you really do not want your emergency room hospital, ER physicians, or radiology bills to be paid by your automobile medical payment coverage. By now, these initial types of medical treatment have already been provided to you. Under the circumstances, you may have limited funds to pay your family doctors and physical therapist, or if necessary, a specialist. You want to save your medical payment coverage for the medical bills you expect to incur **after** your emergency room visit.

9
Do You Have to Reimburse Your Own Insurance Companies?

In many states you may have to reimburse your insurance for bills that they paid related to your accident. This is call "subrogation" and it's one of the ugliest words in your accident case. The good news is that subrogation is not the law in all states. Quickly, subrogation goes like this. You have paid monthly premiums for health insurance, or for medical payment coverage under your automobile insurance policy, for medical bills that you may have resulting from an auto accident. As it is their obligation to do so, your health or auto insurance companies then pay your medical providers.

When you get paid on your claim after a settlement or a trial award, your health insurance and auto insurance companies will want to be reimbursed the payments they made toward your medical bills. You have paid premiums to have health insurance and in turn the health insurance companies paid your medical bills like they were supposed to do. And now they want their money back from you so in effect, you have to pay for your own medical bills. Sound fair? That's one of the reasons why stated earlier that the insurance companies are not your friends.

10
Getting Your Car Fixed

If your car has not been totaled, your insurance company should help you get your car fixed. No matter who is at fault for your accident, if you have the right coverage your own insurance company is obligated to get your car repaired. At worst, your insurance company may have to fight with the insurance company for the driver at fault to get reimbursed for your car repairs. However, different insurance companies will handle your car repairs in different ways. When a property claims adjuster makes contact with you, they should be happy to explain how their repair process works. Some companies will send an adjuster to inspect your car and provide an itemization of the cost to get it repaired. It is then up to you to take that repair estimate to your favorite body shop to see if they will fix your car within the insurance company's proposed range. If your body shop cannot do this, it should be willing to contact your insurance company and work out repairs that satisfy both parties.

Other insurance companies will ask you to get two or three repair estimates from various body shops and submit them to the company for approval. The insurance company and the chosen auto body shop will work out the actual cost of getting your vehicle fixed. This, however, is where things can get scary. On the one hand you have an auto body shop looking to maximize its income. On the other hand you have an insurance company that is willing to have your car repaired, but not necessarily to its original condition, and at the lowest cost possible. It is vital that you have an auto body shop that you know and trust to get your car back to its original condition, or as close as possible, before the accident occurred. What you do not want is an auto body shop willing to do a half-hearted job fixing your car and your insurance company willing to pay cheap for that service.

In the event you own your car without a bank loan or any other lien against it, you may be entitled to the insurance money without having to get it fixed. For the most part, once your insurance company has committed to paying for the repairs to your car, it does not really care whether those repairs are actually done to your car. However, if you have a bank lender that has lien against your car, the bank certainly cares whether those repairs have been made because it does not want its collateral for your loan to lose its full value. Keep in mind that if you do not repair your car, in the future your insurance company may not want to insure that car for its full value since you did not spend its money to get your car fixed.

11
Your Car Is Totaled and You Still Owe Money on It

If your car has been totaled, get ready to take a beating on its value from the insurance company even if it's your own. Insurance companies are obligated only to pay the fair market value of your totaled car; it does not matter how much you still owe the bank on your car loan. Your car's fair market value is determined by the vehicle's year, make, model, mileage, location, overall condition and its variety of features. Your car will have ranges of low, medium and high retail value, as well as a trade in value and perhaps a loan value. For a totaled car, expect the insurance company to offer you somewhere in the low retail value range. If you are still making payments on your car, your lending bank will have a lien against the proceeds from the insurance company. Often times what you owe the bank is more than what the insurance company is willing to give you for your totaled vehicle. If you are willing to accept that amount, you will still owe the bank the balance of your loan.

Yes, you read that correctly! You will get no money from the insurance company, not have a car to drive, and still be making payments to your bank. And guess what else. You still have to go out and buy another car, unless you can find a way to live without one.

You do not have to accept the amount offered to you by an insurance company for your totaled car, but you will have some tough choices to make. Once you receive their first offer, ask the property claims adjuster for a breakdown of how he arrived at your fair market value for your car. But do not be surprised if he is not willing to give it to you. What you are trying to determine is if he missed some of the features on your car that could raise its fair market value. Perhaps the adjuster didn't have the correct year or model when he was determining the value of your car. If you are able to point out some of the deficiencies in his estimates, you may get him to come up a few hundred or even a couple thousand dollars more. But, at some point, the insurance company will draw the line on its offers. Then you will have to decide if you will take that amount or sue to get the full value of your totaled vehicle. You will likely have to find a lawyer to take your case to sue the driver at fault or your own insurance company. Finding that lawyer will be difficult because they won't get paid on a contingency basis but rather on an hourly basis. This will cost you a minimum of a few thousand dollars.

The maximum amount of a claim file suit in small claims court varies from county to county. Your local courthouse will tell you what that amount is, but you can expect that in most places it will not exceed $10,000. You may even stand a fair chance of winning even if the insurance company gets a lawyer involved, which they will. Judges are very aware of insurance companies' low balling people on the value of their cars and, generally, will do what they can to protect the individual against the insurance company and its lawyers. If your dispute is over the maximum amount for small claims court, then you will be involved in a lawsuit of a different kind and one that will be very difficult to win against an insurance company's lawyer.

12
What If the Other Driver Has No Auto Insurance?

It is not the worst thing to happen for your accident claim if the driver at fault has little or no auto insurance. Assuming you have auto insurance coverage on your car, you need two other things:

1. Accept in your own mind that your own insurance company is going to pay on a claim that was caused by someone else.
2. Hope that you have enough uninsured and underinsured motorist coverage to cover all of your damages.

Many people are distressed that even when they are involved in an accident that is not their fault because their own insurance company has to front money to get their car fixed, pay for the loaner car, or get their medical bills paid. Have no fear; your **multi-billion dollar insurance company** will survive paying on your claim.

Why? Because you have been paying premiums, along with hundreds of thousands of other insureds, on a monthly basis in an amount that has been determined by your insurance company to more than adequately cover yours and any others claims they may have to pay on. In the meantime, your insurance company has been investing all of those premiums paid by you and people like you so that instead of merely being a multi-million dollar company, your insurance company may very well be a **multi-billion dollar company**.

Most states may also require you to have the minimum

amount of UM/UIM of about $20,000 for each person and $40,000 per each accident. UM/UIM policy coverages are also typically written as $50,000 or $100,000 per person/per accident. On occasion, some UM/UIM policies will get up in the $250,000 range.

UM/UIM coverage means that if the driver at fault does not have insurance, or does not have enough insurance, to cover your damages, then your UM/UIM policy will kick in and make up the difference. As always, there is a limit to how much your company is willing to pay under your UM/UIM policy and it may be considerably less than what you think.

13
What If You Don't Have Auto Insurance?

Although most if not all states in this country require each driver or automobile to have insurance coverage, that fact that you do not will generally not impact your accident. What is most important is that the driver at fault has insurance.

Your lack of auto insurance is irrelevant to the driver at fault's negligence and his liability for all of your damages. However, if the driver at fault does not have auto insurance and you also do not have auto insurance, then it is not likely that you will recover for the damages to your person or to your vehicle.

If neither you nor the other driver has insurance, then the only way for you to recover is for the driver at fault to have enough money to pay for your damages. This probably will not happen considering that if the driver at fault had money to begin with, then they most likely would have paid for auto insurance.

14
Photographs and Witnesses

As soon as you can, get photographs of your injuries, even if you're in the hospital. It sounds a bit cheesy to be taking pictures of yourself or a loved at a time like this, but it is very important to document the injuries and the trauma from the time of the accident onwards. Besides the injury itself, photographs of a client/patient demonstrate the pain and suffering a person is going through and will have a huge impact on both the adjuster for the insurance company and if necessary, on a jury at trial.

Also, take pictures of your car if there is a lot of damages or something unique about your accident that you think needs to be documented. Truth be told, the amount of damage to your vehicle has very little to do with the injuries to the people inside of it at the time of the accident. But insurance companies like to make a connection between extensive property damage and a person's physical injuries. So, if you do have extensive damage to your car, photographs can help your case. On the other hand, if you car shows little or no damage then not only will photographs do you no good, but you'll also put your lawyer in the position of having to argue how you could be seriously injured if your car has so little damage to it.

If there are witnesses to your accident, hopefully the investigating police officer will have marked down their names and contact information in the Traffic Accident Report. It is not recommended that you contact witnesses yourself; leave this task to your lawyer.

15
What Is Your Case Worth?

Until at least you have stopped being treated for your injuries, determining the value of your case is a bit difficult. Learning how to value your case is, in part, why lawyers went to law school and spent years in training, experience, and staying current on laws and trends that affect your case. In the golden days, soft tissue injury claims settled like clockwork for three times the medical bills and other damages. This is simply not the case anymore and it has nothing to do with a great economy.

Unfortunately, there are so many factors involved evaluating an injury claim, that it is impossible for any other lawyer to tell you with any certainty the value of your case until having all of the necessary information. It can only be said that most people either grossly under value, or terribly over value, their injury claims.

16
How Long Will Your Case Take?

Although there are some exceptions, generally your case will not settle or you will not be awarded damages until after your medical treatment is completed. To some degree whether or not your injuries have been fully healed or if you have scars from your accident has a bearing on the value of your case. Two exceptions to this general rule are if:

1. You will need long-term medical treatment in the future, or
2. There is a limited amount of insurance or assets to recover from the driver at fault as compensation for your damages.

In either case, there is nothing fast about recovering damages for you injuries after an accident. Injury settlements or awards are one of those things in life that you should not make too many plans for until you are very close to receiving your money.

In fact, the "deny and delay" tactic is one commonly used by insurance companies to get injured victims to settle their cases for low amounts. Insurance companies know that accidents can put a financial strain on injured people and will always try "waiting" people out in order to pay less money on claim. All the while, the insurance companies know that the injured person's lawyers are not allowed to pay their client's bills, loan them money, or guarantee their loans to help them get by financially until their claim is resolved.

17
Do You Have to Settle Your Case?

You do not have to settle your case if you do not want to. There is no one that can force your hand to sign a Release from an insurance company, not even your lawyer. If you want to have a trial before a judge or jury then you may get your wish if you can find the right lawyer to take your case.

Now, at some point common sense and reason should come into your thinking. It makes no sense to be offered fair amount of money to settle your case, only to insist on more because you want a trial no matter how many dollars are offered to you. If you are being unreasonable in your demands and unless you are willing to pay attorney fees out of your own pocket on a per hour basis, you will have a difficult time finding a lawyer to take your case all the way to trial.

But, do keep in mind that once you sign a Release and finally settle your case, you will not be able to come back later and get more money out of the driver at fault or their insurance company.

18
Do You Have to Go to Trial? With a Jury?

No one, not even your well-meaning, super aggressive lawyer can force you to go to trial. Still, once your lawyer takes your case, in their mind they should be preparing your file as if it will go to trial. But the truth is probably more than 90% of the accident claims that occur are settled without the parties having to go near a courthouse. That does not mean you or your lawyer do not want to have a trial, just that most likely your case will work out to where your satisfied with the money in your pocket after all fees, costs, and medical bills have been paid.

Your lawyer can't force you to go to trial. On the other hand, within reason, if you want your day in court then you are entitled to it. Hopefully, your common sense and some good advice will make your decisions for trial or settlement easier than you think.

If you do go to trial, will it be with a jury or the judge making the decision. In most states, if all parties agree then the judge can make the decisions on liability and damages in your case. This is known as a bench trial. But if one party wants to have a jury trial in your accident case, then they will be entitled to have liability and damages decided by twelve people.

Depending on the court jurisdiction and the presiding judge, sometimes the plaintiff in the case, that is, the injured party, would be very happy with a bench trial instead of a jury trial. But almost always the defendants in the case, who caused the accident, will want a jury trial instead of a bench trial.

19
Drunk Driver Accidents

Many accidents these days are caused by drivers under the influence of alcohol or drugs. All businesses serving alcohol should have Dram Shop Insurance. If you've been injured by a drunk driver you may also have a claim against the bar or restaurant that kept serving their customer while they should have known that driver was intoxicated.

Negligent drivers under the influence of alcohol or drugs make insurance companies nervous and they will almost always pay in the higher range of a claim's value. Why? Insurance companies simply cannot afford to let a jury get angry over a drunk driver and award an injured person with a huge verdict. Sometimes a huge verdict is just what needs to happen to send a message about drunk driving; other times that gamble at trial is not worth your risk.

Either way, be smart about your claim. And do what's best for yourself and your love ones.

20
Criminal Charges Against the Drunk Driver

There are many times when the driver at fault in your accident is charged with traffic or criminal citations. At the very least, if the other party receives a citation, it gets the adjuster for their insurance company at least thinking that their insured was at fault for your injuries and damages. If the driver at fault ends up being convicted for the citations, then all the better for you if there is a dispute over liability or if your case ends up in a trial.

Sometimes, if the driver at fault was under the influence of alcohol or drugs and people are seriously injured, the County Prosecutor may file additional criminal charges against the other driver; charges above and beyond simple traffic citations. These types of criminal charges against the driver at fault makes insurance companies scared to let your case go to trial and it becomes very likely that you will settle at a high value.

Also, remember that only the government attorneys can prosecute and punish the driver at fault for his criminal actions. The attorney you hire represents you against the driver at fault for civil actions and is hired primarily to get you money for your injuries and damages.

21
What Happens if a Minor Was Hurt in the Accident?

When it comes to accident cases, a minor has all the same rights and protections as would an adult under the same circumstances. For that matter, a minor has even more rights and protections than would an adult. For example, with adults many injury cases have a two-year deadline to file a lawsuit, otherwise the injured person loses most their rights to be compensated for their damages. This is called a statute of limitations. But with a minor, that two-year statute of limitations does not even start until the minor reaches the age of 18 years. So in reality, a minor has until they are 20 years old to file a lawsuit for their injuries. Be aware, though, different states and different types of injuries can have different statutes of limitations. That statute of limitations can sometimes be as short as one year or even six months.

There is one more thing to keep in mind about accidents involving minors. Depending on the amount of the settlement or award that a minor may receive from an accident, state laws may require court approval or that a guardianship bank account be established. In these situations it will take a court order for any of the money to be spent. This is all to make sure that a minor's best interests are being served and that the money from their accident is used only for the benefit of the minor.

22
Statutes of Limitation Can Stop Your Claim

A statute of limitations is a deadline that one must file a lawsuit with the appropriate court or else be at great risk that the injured party may never be able to recover money for their injuries and damages. You must either accept a final settlement offer, or file a lawsuit with the court, within the time periods required by the appropriate statutes of limitations. The statute of limitations involving accidents are different from State to State, but very common ones are as follows:

1. For bodily and personal injury claims, the statute of limitations is:

    a. Within **2 years** from the date of the accident; or

    b. If your accident was caused by a government employee or government related, then the statute of limitations is **1 year** from the date of the accident; or

    c. Within **2 years** from the date of your 18th birthday if you were under age 18 when the accident occurred, even if the accident was government related.

2. For property damage claims the statute of limitations is within 5 years from the date of the accident, regardless of your age at the time the accident occurred.

If you fail to accept a final settlement offer or file a lawsuit before the statute of limitations ends, you may jeopardize your right to receive any settlement at all.

Again, different states and different types of injuries can have different statutes of limitations. That statute of limitations can sometimes be as short as one year or even six months. The safest thing to do is check with an attorney as soon as possible so that a statute of limitations does not defeat your claim.

23
What Are the Damages in Your Case?

If you've been in an accident, depending on your types of injuries and how severe you've been hurt, you may recover damages for:

1. Past and future medical bills
2. Mental anguish
3. Emotional distress
4. Pain and suffering
5. Loss of companionship, love, counseling
6. Grief and sorrow
7. Disfigurement/scarring
8. Loss of consortium
9. Past and future lost wages
10. Job rehabilitation
11. Property replacement or repairs
12. Punitive damages

Fortunately, or perhaps unfortunately, there is no set dollar value for any of the different types of damages in this list. In one case very high medical bills may lead to a very high value of a claim. In another case, the medical bills may be very low, but the pain and suffering or loss of companionship resulting from the accident may make the damages very high. Injury cases are like fingerprints. No two injury claims are exactly alike and the value of each is normally only determined on a case-by-case basis.

24
What You Must Know about the Insurance Companies

1. Insurance companies are not in the business of paying claims such as yours.
2. Insurance companies are not going to pay your medical bills. If they do, it's probably because they're taking advantage of you and want to close out your file as soon as possible.
3. Insurance companies will sometimes delay your claim along until you get tired of dealing with it the statute of limitations has passed.
4. Insurance companies will threaten to "close their file" when they can't get you to agree to their offer. So long as the statute of limitations hasn't passed, it means nothing to you if the insurance company closes its files.
5. Insurance companies don't care what you learn about how injury claims are processed, so long as you don't hire a lawyer to work through all the hassles for you.
6. Insurance companies will settle your case and then send you a check with the names of other people and organizations on it, like hospitals, doctors, and Medicare. Then it's up to you to try and get those other parties to sign off on your check so you can spend your money. Good luck with that.
7. Insurance companies will ask to you sign forms so they can get copies of your medical records that have nothing to do with your accident. It's not so much that they're being nosey; it's that they're trying to create delays and find ways to argue deny your claim because of prior injuries or treatment.
8. Insurance companies will make low ball offers on

your car repairs because they're gambling there's not enough money worth your filing a lawsuit over.
9. Soon after an accident, the adjuster for the insurance company will set a "reserve" indicating how much it might have to pay you for your claim. Adjusters hate to increase these reserves and will not do so without an extremely good reason, and even then they have to explain why to their supervisors.
10. Once a claimant hires an attorney, the insurance adjuster will increase their "reserves" by two, three, or even more times their original estimate of the value of your case.
11. Don't speak to any insurance company, even your own, without first talking to your lawyer.

25
Do You Really Need a Lawyer for Your Accident Case?

When you read about insurance companies that work against you and try to minimize your claim, you will not only want a lawyer for your accident, you will need one to get you through what could end up being a very difficult time in your life. Although it's not a complete list, the following are a few things you might expect your lawyer to do in your accident case:

1. Obtain the official Crash Report from the police.
2. Acquire photographs of the vehicles and crash site.
3. Interview witnesses.
4. Order copies of your medical records and bills.
5. Retain an accident reconstruction expert, if necessary.
6. Gather any other documents or evidence to support your claim and damages.
7. Deal with the other driver's insurance company so you don't have to.
8. Help get your medical bills paid by any available insurance.
9. Handle any problems with Medicare and Medicaid.
10. Reduce or eliminate liens against your settlement or trial award.
11. File a lawsuit, if necessary.
12. Prepare you to give a statement to the opposing party.
13. File appropriate motions with the Court.
14. Prepare you for trial, if one is necessary.
15. Have your case ready for trial.
16. Take your case through a verdict in your favor.

In the end, you may not want to go to a lawyer for your accident case, just like you don't want to go to the dentist for a toothache. But meeting a lawyer for your accident case will be a painless appointment, will immediately relieve some of your concerns and make you much happier in the long run. So while you may not want to go to lawyer, you sure do need to see one as soon as possible.

26
How Do You Pay a Lawyer to Take Your Case?

In a personal injury case that arises out of an auto accident, your lawyer should be paid on a contingency fee basis. Meaning, your lawyer will get paid his attorney fees only if he is able to get you a settlement or trial verdict in your favor. If your lawyer does not get you a settlement or an award, then you should not expect to have any attorney fees. Usually, the attorney fees for an accident case will be 33% of the gross amount your attorney may recover on your behalf. This 33% in attorney fees typically comes before any reduction for medical bills, reimbursement of costs, or any setoffs to other parties. Some attorneys will increase their percentage in the event of a second trial or an appeal of a bad decision in the trial court.

You should expect that your attorney will advance costs for your medical records, police reports, filing fees, depositions, expert witness fees, and more expenses related to your case. Reimbursement of these advanced costs will come out of your settlement or award after a trial. If you do not get a settlement or award, some attorneys will waive your advanced costs; others will still expect you to pay them back.

Your attorney should consult with you in before spending large sums on your case, such as expert witness fees. If your case is one of relatively low risk with the potential for a high return in money damages, then your lawyer will not ask you for advanced payment of the expensive case costs. But if your case involves a close call on liability, or it has relatively low value, then don't expect your lawyer to gamble thousands of his own dollars in costs and expenses.

Most importantly, get your lawyer's thoughts on fees and costs up front. Experienced personal injury lawyers will be able to let you know fairly early on your case whether they will be willing to advance your costs throughout their representation. Some lawyers will not even take your case if they are not 100% convinced that they will get you a satisfactory settlement or award that more than covers your reasonable damages, medical bills, attorney's fees, and costs.

27

Should You Tell Your Lawyer Everything about Your Case?

Without question or hesitation, you should tell your lawyer everything—at least about your case and injuries. Whatever you think you did wrong or is bad about your case now, it will be ten times worse if you keep it a secret, only to have it come spilling out come trial time. The sooner you can tell your lawyer the bad parts of your case, the sooner he can start planning ahead to minimize their affects. If you have secrets about your case but your lawyer hasn't asked you the right question for you to bring up the matter, do not hesitate to start talking about it on your own. Put your hand up and tell your lawyer you have something important that may hurt your case. I guarantee you that you will have that lawyer's full attention; so take the opportunity and let it all pour out.

Truth be known, most of what people think is bad for their case turns out to be not that damaging from a lawyer's view. Or, even if it is, at least telling your lawyer early on gives him time to come up with an ethical game plan to still protect the value of your case—warts and all. At the worst, if there is something that absolutely destroys your case, wouldn't you rather want to know early on in your case instead of keeping secrets so that you end up wasting a lot of time and stress on false hopes?

28
At Least Twelve Things You Should Expect from Your Injury Lawyer

1. A willingness to answer any of your questions.
2. Patience in answering your questions.
3. Return your phone calls and emails within at least a day or two.
4. Settle your case only with your permission.
5. Prepare you to give a statement to the opposing attorney.
6. Prepare you for trial.
7. Membership in the American Association for Justice.
8. Membership in their State's Trial Lawyer Association.
9. Respect.
10. Personal attention from a licensed attorney.
11. An itemization of all the costs in your case.
12. Honest and straightforward advice, even if it's not what you want to hear, but need to hear.

29
Five Things You Normally Won't Be Told about Injury Lawyers

1. Free Consultations by Lawyers

Whenever you hear or read of a lawyer offering a Free Consultation, your response should be something like, "Big Deal." When it comes to accident cases, all lawyers should be willing to give you a free consultation, especially since their attorney's fees are going to be paid on a contingency basis. If a lawyer is not willing to give you a free consultation on your accident case, then either you have an inexperienced injury lawyer or that lawyer thinks your case is so weak he doesn't really want to take you on as a client.

2. No Recovery, No Lawyer Fees

Many lawyer advertisements will make a big deal pointing out that if you don't recover any money then you will not have any attorney's fees. Well I should hope not. Why should you have to pay your lawyer any attorney's fees in an injury case if you did not win? Experienced injury lawyers will almost always take your case on a contingency basis; so if you don't have any recovery you will not have any attorney fees. This is standard practice for personal injury cases and lawyers advertising NO RECOVERY, NO FEES are only pretending to offer their clients a special benefit.

3. We Fight the Big Insurance Companies

Well, what personal injury lawyer doesn't fight the big insurance companies? Compared to even the largest injury law firms, the smaller insurance companies are huge companies of bureaucratic red tape designed to make their shareholders money, not pay out on claims. All accident lawyers fight the big insurance companies. Why? Because there really are no small insurance companies.

4. Serious Lawyers for Serious Cases

What exactly is a serious case? To anyone injured from an accident, their case is certainly serious to them. But what does their lawyer think is a serious injury? Does there need to be a broken bone? The loss of a limb? Or even a death? It would appear so, since some lawyers only want injury cases are "serious" enough for them, and that may not include your case. Does that mean that these lawyers don't even want to talk to you about your injury case? Or just that they won't be serious about your case, even if you are their client? This doesn't mean that every lawyer should be willing to take your case no matter how bad your injury may or may not be; but you shouldn't limit yourself to seeking out the so called "serious lawyers".

5. Aggressive, Dedicated, and Justice-Seeking Lawyers

If a lawyer has to market to you that they are aggressive, dedicated and seeks justice, then the first thing you might ask yourself is: Why do they feel the need to tell me these things? Is there some reason that people don't think this particular lawyer is aggressive, dedicated or seeks justice? Is there some reason this lawyer needs to stress these qualities? Are not most, if not all, lawyers dedicated and seek justice?

30
Are People These Days Too Lawsuit Happy?

Well, if you think so, you're not alone; but most of the people who think like this have never been in an accident or have never seen a loved one seriously injured by someone else's negligence. The vast majority of people in a serious accident would prefer the accident never have happened rather than to have whatever money they received from their claim.

So, do you really want to give up on thousands of dollars for someone else's principles and to save money for a multi-billion dollar insurance company? Besides, the vast majority of accident cases settle before filing a lawsuit is even necessary.

31
This Book Does Not Offer Legal Advice

The information and materials in this book are provided for general informational purposes only and are not intended to be legal advice. The law changes frequently and varies from jurisdiction to jurisdiction. Being general in nature, the information and materials provided may not apply to any specific factual and/or legal set of circumstances. No attorney-client relationship is formed nor should any such relationship be implied.

Nothing in this book is intended to substitute for the advice of an attorney, especially an attorney licensed in your jurisdiction. If you require legal advice, please consult with a competent attorney licensed to practice in your jurisdiction.

32

The Ten Worst Insurance Companies in America and the Wealth of the Insurance Industry

1. Allstate: The poster child for insurance industry greed; the number of complaints filed against Allstate are greater than those of almost all its major competitors combined.
2. Unum: One of the nation's leading disability insurers, with a long reputation for unfairly denying and delaying claims.
3. AIG: The world's biggest insurer, but with a long history of claims-handling abuses.
4. State Farm: The nation's biggest property casualty insurance company, with a reputation for its deny and delay tactics.
5. Conseco: Sells long term care policies with a reputation of delaying claims until the insured has died.
6. WellPoint: Reportedly routinely cancels the policies of pregnant women and chronically ill patients.
7. Farmers: Rewarded adjusters who met low claim payment goals.
8. United Health: Plagued by accusations of greed so rampant that it puts patients at risk.
9. Torchmark: Has been criticized for a variety of transgressions, among them charging minority policyholders more than whites.
10. Liberty Mutual: Adopted a policy of deny, delay, and defend; cited by regulators for systematic bid rigging.

The insurance industry in the United States received over $1 trillion dollars annually in premiums.

The insurance industry in the United States has over $3.8 trillion dollars in assets, which is greater than the Gross Domestic Products of all countries in the world except the U.S. and Japan.

For a recent 10 year period, the property/casualty insurance industry has enjoyed average profits of over $30 billion per year.

Printed with permission from the source, American Association for Justice: *The Ten Worst Insurance Companies in America: How They Raise Premiums, Deny Claims, and Refuse Insurance to Those Who Need it Most*, American Association for Justice.
www.justice.org/docs/tenworstinsurancecompanies.pdf.

33
About the Author

Steve Giacoletto has been representing persons injured in accidents since 1990. His region-wide law practice is based out of Collinsville, Illinois, and consists primarily of victims from auto accidents, truck accidents, and premises liability falls. For more information about finding an experienced injury and wrongful death lawyer, please visit his website at www.giaclaw.com where you can get much more information in the videos and blogs about auto, truck, and wrongful death accidents.

Giacoletto Law Firm
1601 Vandalia Street
Collinsville, IL 62234
Phone: (618) 346-8841
Toll Free: (866) 346-8841
Fax: (618) 346-8843
sgiacoletto@scglawoffice.com
www.scglawoffice.com

www.ingramcontent.com/pod-product-compliance
Lightning Source LLC
Chambersburg PA
CBHW071636170526
45166CB00003B/1345